I0441407

The Constitution of the United States

America's Owner's Manual

James Magee

Other books by this author can be found at www.littrivia.com

Preface

The Constitution of the United States consists of
150 questions and answers which examine the entire
history of the Constitution from the ideas that helped
shape it and the events leading to its ratification. This
book will assist the reader in understanding the processes
of thought that compelled the Constitutions writers along
with the Constitution's development and interpretation
once it was enacted. The constitution should be viewed
as both an original document and a "living" document
that has undergone many changes over time through the
addition of amendments.

The Constitution of the United States has a definite
structure and format. There are two questions per page
with their answers on the following page. Each of these
answers also provides additional *trivia* information. An
added benefit is that this book can be opened to any page
at any time. Questions are randomly presented and span
the entire history of the Constitution.

"The Constitution is America's Owner's Manual"

Anonymous

QUESTION # 1

What are the official dates that we recognize regarding the Constitution of the United States when we discuss its creation and ratification?

QUESTION # 2

Where does the Constitution of the United States reside at the present time?

ANSWER # 1

The Constitution was created on
September 17, 1787 and it was ratified on
June 21, 1788.

ANSWER # 2

The Constitution of the United States
resides in the National Archives and
Records Administration in Washington,
D.C.

QUESTION # 3

Who are the authors of the Constitution of
the United States?

QUESTION # 4

How many of the 74 deputies (delegates)
appointed to the Philadelphia Convention
signed the Constitution of the United
States?

ANSWER # 3

The authors of the Constitution of the
United States were the deputies
(delegates) to the Constitutional
Convention in Pennsylvania. It is also
referred to as the Philadelphia
Convention.

ANSWER # 4

The Constitution of the United States was
signed by 39 out of the 74 appointees and
55 attending deputies (delegates) who
attended the Constitutional Convention in
Philadelphia, Pennsylvania which was
also known as the Philadelphia
Convention..

QUESTION # 5

What was the purpose of the Constitution of the United States after it was ratified on June 21, 1788?

QUESTION # 6

How was the Constitution of the United States ratified in every state?

ANSWER # 5

The Constitution of the United States acted as a national constitution. It replaced the Articles of Confederation (and Perpetual Union) which was drafted by a committee in June, 1776 during the Second Continental Congress. The Articles had legally established the union of the States.

ANSWER # 6

The Constitution was ratified at conventions in each U. S. state in the name of "The People."

QUESTION # 7

How many amendments have there been
to the Constitution of the United States?

QUESTION # 8

How should "constitution" be defined?

ANSWER # 7

There have been 27 amendments to the
Constitution of the United States.

ANSWER # 8

A constitution embodies the fundamental principles of a
government. Our constitution, adopted by the sovereign
power, is amendable by that power only. To the
constitution all laws, executive actions, and, judicial
decisions must conform, as it is the creator of the powers
exercised by the departments of government. (An excerpt
from *The Story of the Constitution* by Sol Bloom – see
Bibliography)

QUESTION # 9

Who must vote on an amendment for its enactment into law?

QUESTION # 10

What are the minimum margins needed for an amendment to be passed?

?

ANSWER # 9

In order for an amendment to pass and be enacted into law, a vote must be conducted in the House of Representatives and Senate. Once this is completed, the voting precedes to the states in the Union.

ANSWER # 10

The minimum margin needed for an amendment to pass is 2/3 majority of the House and Senate along with 3/4 majority of the states in the Union.

QUESTION # 11

Is the President's signature needed for an amendment to pass into law?

QUESTION # 12

Who is referred to as the "Father of the Constitution?"

ANSWER # 11

In order for an amendment to pass into law, the President's signature is not needed.

ANSWER # 12

James Madison is referred to as the "Father of the Constitution."

QUESTION # 13

What is the purpose of each of the three branches of government: the Legislative Branch, the Executive Branch and the Judicial Branch?

QUESTION # 14

How does power flow based on the Declaration of Independence and the Constitution of the United States?

ANSWER # 13

The Legislative Branch of the government makes laws, the Executive Branch enforces the laws and the Judicial Branch interprets the laws.

ANSWER # 14

The Declaration of Independence and the Constitution of the United States imply that power flows first from God to the people and then to the elected officials.

QUESTION # 15

Why are checks and balances necessary within the government of the United States?

QUESTION # 16

Which two Founding Fathers who became President stopped speaking to each other until they were in old age – only to then die hours apart of each other on July 4th, 1826?

ANSWER # 15

Checks and balances within the government prevent any one branch of government from over powering any other branch of government.

ANSWER # 16

Thomas Jefferson and John Adams reconciled in old age only to die hours apart on Independence Day in 1826.

QUESTION # 17

When did the United States create an
Income Tax?

QUESTION # 18

What specific power does a Supreme
Court Justice have dating back to the
Marbury versus Madison Supreme Court
case? This landmark case formed the
basis for judicial review under Article III
of the Constitution.

ANSWER # 17

The Income Tax was a result of the 16th Amendment in 1913. It allowed the Congress to levy this tax without apportioning it amongst the states or basing it on Census results.

ANSWER # 18

Supreme Court Justices have the power to declare a law as "unconstitutional" based on the landmark case Marbury versus Madison where John Marbury did not receive a mailed commission to be the Justice of the Peace in the District of Columbia as appointed by President John Adams.

QUESTION # 19

Which other President and Founding Father also died on Independence Day like Thomas Jefferson and John Adams who died hours apart on July 4th, 1826.

QUESTION # 20

What are Bills of Attainder?

ANSWER # 19

James Monroe died on July 4th, 1831 (Independence Day) just as Thomas Jefferson and John Adams did in 1826.

ANSWER # 20

A Bill of Attainder is an act of the legislature accusing a person or group of persons to be guilty of some crime and punishing them without benefit of a trial.

QUESTION # 21

Where does the Constitution of the
United States prevent any Bills of
Attainder?

QUESTION # 22

What is the short version of the 2nd
Amendment (Bill of Rights)?

ANSWER # 21

Article I, sec 9 of the Constitution prevents Bill of Attainder in the federal government while Article I, sec 10 prevents Bills of Attainder on a state level.

ANSWER # 22

The short version of the 2rd Amendment (Bill of Rights) is that citizens have the right to bear arms.

QUESTION # 23

What is the short version of the 3rd Amendment (Bill of Rights)?

QUESTION # 24

According to the Constitution of the United States, what is the minimum infraction required for impeachment of a Judge?

ANSWER # 23

The short version of the 3rd Amendment (Bill of Rights) is that citizens can refuse to quarter soldiers.

ANSWER # 24

According to Article 3, Section 1 of the Constitution of the United States, the minimum infraction required for impeachment of a Judge is bad behavior.

QUESTION # 25

What is the short version of the 4th
Amendment (Bill of Rights)?

QUESTION # 26

What is the short version of the 5th
Amendment (Bill of Rights)?

ANSWER # 25

The short version of the 4ᵗʰ Amendment (Bill of Rights) is that a search warrant is necessary for seizure and search.

ANSWER # 26

The short version of the 5ᵗʰ Amendment (Bill of Rights) is that citizens have a right to a grand jury, are protected against double jeopardy (not tried twice for the same crime), are protected against self-incrimination, and must be accused of a crime and have the right to remain silent.

QUESTION # 27

Does the Constitution of the United States allow the government to take private property for public use?

QUESTION # 28

What is the short version of the 6th Amendment (Bill of Rights)?

ANSWER # 27

According to the 5th Amendment (Bill of Rights) of the Constitution of the United States, the government is permitted to take private property for public use providing that the owner is paid a fair price for it.

ANSWER # 28

The short version of the 6th Amendment (Bill of Rights) is that citizens have a right to a fair and speedy trial.

QUESTION # 29

What is the short version of the 1st
Amendment (Bill of Rights)?

QUESTION # 30

Does the Constitution of the United
States specifically forbid slavery or
involuntary servitude?

ANSWER # 29

The short version of the 1st Amendment (Bill of Rights) is that all citizens are guaranteed five basic freedoms: freedom of speech, freedom of religion, freedom of press, freedom of assembly and freedom to petition.

ANSWER # 30

According to the 13th Amendment, the federal government forbids slavery or involuntary servitude except as a punishment for a crime.

QUESTION # 31

Is the promotion of the arts and sciences specifically mentioned in the Constitution of the United States?

QUESTION # 32

What is the short version of the 7th Amendment?

ANSWER # 31

In Article 1, Section 8 of the Constitution of the United States, Congress has the power to give authors and inventors exclusive rights to their works.

ANSWER # 32

The short version of the 7th Amendment is that citizens have the right to a trial by jury in a non-criminal case.

QUESTION # 33

What is the short version of the 8th Amendment?

QUESTION # 34

How many Cabinet members are there and are they mentioned in the Constitution?

ANSWER # 33

The short version of the 8th Amendment is that all citizens are protected from any cruel and unusual punishments.

ANSWER # 34

The 15 members of the Cabinet are department heads who are appointed by the President. They are not specifically mentioned in the Constitution.

QUESTION # 35

What is the short version of the 9th Amendment?

QUESTION # 36

What is the short version of the 10th Amendment?

ANSWER # 35

The short version of the 9th Amendment is that this amendment deals with people's rights that are specifically enumerated within the Constitution. If a right is not mentioned, it does not follow that the people forfeit that right to the federal government.

ANSWER # 36

The short version of the 10 Amendment is that it deals with state's rights.

QUESTION # 37

What is the enigma attached to the 9th Amendment that has been reflected both in its language and its history?

QUESTION # 38

Who was the President of the Philadelphia Convention that met in Philadelphia, Pennsylvania?

ANSWER # 37

The enigmatic wording of the 9th Amendment was an outgrowth of the friction and opposition between the Federalists and the Anti-federalists. The power of the central (Federal) government or the power of the States was at risk. No one wanted to cede control or have it stolen from them in the unseen future. This was a catch-all, compromising way to keeping the door open so that the people's rights that were not enumerated in the 1st eight amendments could be declared later.

ANSWER # 38

The President of the Philadelphia Convention that met in Philadelphia, Pennsylvania was George Washington who would eventually become the 1st President of the United States.

QUESTION # 39

Which state was the only state not to attend the Constitutional Congress?

QUESTION # 40

Which vote actually elects the President of the United States – the electoral vote or the popular vote?

ANSWER # 39

Rhode Island (& Providence Plantations) was the only state that did not send any deputies (delegates) to the Convention. Like Patrick Henry, the politicians of Rhode Island feared that the purpose of the Convention was to create a powerful Central government.

ANSWER # 40

The President of the United States is actually elected by the electoral vote that is computed by the Electoral College.

QUESTION # 41

What amendment replaced Article III, Section 1, and clause 3 and changed how we elect the President and Vice President of the United States?

QUESTION # 42

Do U.S. Territories have representatives in the Electoral College which is a form of indirect election based on Article II, sec. 1, cl. 2 of the Constitution of the United States?

ANSWER # 41

Article III, Section 1, Clause 3 was replaced by the 12th Amendment which changed how the Electoral College functioned due to the Elections of 1796 and 1800.

ANSWER # 42

U.S. Territories do not have any representatives in the Electoral College which has had 538 electors in every presidential election since 1964. The 23rd Amendment was enacted to specify how many electors the District of Columbia would be permitted.

QUESTION # 43

How was the problem of the large states versus the small states and the differences in population handled by the Founding Fathers?

QUESTION # 44

What part or parts of the Constitution of the United States determine the line of succession if the President dies in office?

ANSWER # 43

The Virginia and the New Jersey Plans were offered to resolve size and population differences of the states. Eventually, the deputies (delegates) agreed on the Connecticut Compromise that led to our present-day system where population is used to fill the House with two Senators per state.

ANSWER # 44

Article 2, Section 1 along with amendments 20 and 25 determine by law that the line of succession after the President dies in office should be Vice President, Speaker of the House, President Pro Tempore of the Senate, Secretary of State, Secretary of the Treasury, Secretary of Defense, Attorney General, etc.

QUESTION # 45

What is an impeachment and does it lead
to removal from office?

QUESTION # 46

How many Presidents have gone through
the entire process of an impeachment
from beginning to end and who were
they?

ANSWER # 45

Impeachment is a formal process where an official is accused of wrongdoing and unlawful activity. It does not necessarily mean that an official who is accused must be removed from office. It is like an indictment in a criminal action.

ANSWER # 46

There were only two Presidents who went through the entire process of an impeachment. They were President William Jefferson "Bill" Clinton (1993-2001) and President Andrew Johnson (1865-1869).

QUESTION # 47

What are the first ten amendments to the Constitution of the United States called?

QUESTION # 48

What is the historical development of the day known to us as Inauguration Day when the President takes the oath of office?

ANSWER # 47

The first ten amendments to the Constitution of the United States are called the Bill of Rights. They were called the Bill of Rights by the Founding Fathers because they provided protection over the rights that citizens had.

ANSWER # 48

Inauguration Day (the day that the President takes the oath of affirmation as directed by the Constitution) was on March 4th from 1793 to 1933. The 20th Amendment specified that January 20th would be the new day when the President would be sworn in by a Supreme Court Justice.

QUESTION # 49

What did the 20th Amendment deal with?

QUESTION # 50

What name currently identifies the building where the Constitutional Convention (1787) was held in Philadelphia, Pennsylvania?

ANSWER # 49

The 20th Amendment deals with the beginning and endings of the terms of office regarding federal officials. It also discusses the circumstances surrounding the absence of a President-Elect.

ANSWER # 50

The current name of the building where the Constitutional Convention (1787) was held in Philadelphia is now known as Independence Hall.

QUESTION # 51

Unlike the First Continental Congress
(1774) which was attended by 54 delegates
from 12 states, how did the Constitution
Convention (1787) fare regarding
attendance?

QUESTION # 52

Aside from the 27 Amendments that exist,
how many parts and Articles exist in the
Constitution?

ANSWER # 51

Rhode Island never attended the Constitutional Convention? New Hampshire's deputies arrived late which meant that there were never more than 11 states present at any one time. Because the other two delegates left without signing, Alexander Hamilton did not sign until later.

ANSWER # 52

There are 3 parts to the Constitution which have 7 Articles.

QUESTION # 53

What was the average age of the deputies (delegates) that attended the Constitutional Convention? Who was the oldest delegate and who was the youngest delegate?

QUESTION # 54

How were the deputies (delegates) chosen as representatives of their respective (Colonies) states?

ANSWER # 53

The average age of the deputies (delegates) that attended the Constitutional Convention was 44 years of age. Benjamin Franklin was the oldest member at age 81 while the youngest delegate was Jonathan Dayton from New Jersey at the age of 26.

ANSWER # 54

The deputies (delegates) to the Constitutional Convention were appointed by the state legislatures of their respective (Colonies) States.

QUESTION # 55

Was there any restriction on the number of deputies (delegates) that could be sent by any Colony (State)?

QUESTION # 56

How many deputies (delegates) were appointed to the Constitutional Convention even though only 55 attended?

ANSWER # 55

There was no restriction on how many deputies could be sent by each State. Even though New York sent three deputies, only Alexander Hamilton signed the Constitution and that was later. While New York only had his signature, most of the other States that signed had at least two signatures.

ANSWER # 56

There were 74 deputies (delegates) appointed by 12 of the 13 colonies who were supposed to attend the Constitutional Convention. Rhode Island believed that the convention was just a ploy for the federal government to wrest control over the smaller states.

QUESTION # 57

How long did it take to draft the
Constitution of the United States?

QUESTION # 58

What was the Virginia Plan and who
presented it to the Constitutional
Convention?

ANSWER # 57

The drafting of the Constitution took less than a 100 working days.

ANSWER # 58

The Virginia Plan was presented by Governor Edmund Randolph of Virginia to the delegates of the Philadelphia Convention after it was drafted by James Madison. It proposed a bicameral House where the lower House would elect the upper House after it was first elected by a proportionate vote.

QUESTION # 59

What was the New Jersey Plan - which considered the smaller States plight when population provided unequal representation - and which deputy submitted it to the Constitutional Convention?

QUESTION # 60

How many delegates out of the 55 who attended the Constitutional Convention studied law or were lawyers?

ANSWER # 59

The New Jersey Plan was submitted soon after the Virginia Plan was presented the Virginia Plan. It sought to resolve the bias that would arise when the population of the larger States allocated them more delegates. Both plans eventually helped the acceptance of the Connecticut Compromise.

ANSWER # 60

Out of the 55 delegates that attended the Constitutional Convention, 34 had studied law at one time or another (some were actual lawyers who practiced law like Alexander Hamilton).

QUESTION # 61

How many of the members of the
Continental Congress (1774-1789 were
part of the 55 deputies to the Philadelphia
Convention (May 25 – September 17,
1787)?

QUESTION # 62

By what titles were the attendees to the
Constitutional Convention in
Philadelphia known in 1787?

ANSWER # 61

Forty of the deputies that were members
of the Continental Congress became part
of the 55 deputies that attended the
Philadelphia Convention. Some of the
earlier attendees chose to seek positions
in State government.

ANSWER # 62

The attendees at the Philadelphia
Convention were referred to as deputies,
delegates and commissioners.
Eventually, delegates won out. George
Washington signed documents there as
the "deputy from Virginia."

QUESTION # 63

Before the Constitution was ratified in
1788, how were Senators elected?

QUESTION # 64

What sources had the greatest influence
upon the philosophy that pervaded the
thoughts of the attendees at the
Constitutional Convention?

ANSWER # 63

Before the Constitution was ratified, Senators were installed in their office by a vote of the state legislatures.

ANSWER # 64

Some significant influences on the philosophy and thinking of the attendees were a book written by the French philosopher, Montesquieu, titled *Spirit of the Laws* (1748) and a book titled *Two Treatises on Government* by the English philosopher, John Locke.

QUESTION # 65

Were there any deputies who never attended the meetings that were held at the Constitutional Convention?

QUESTION # 66

Who was referred to as the "Sage of the Constitution?"

ANSWER # 65

There were **19** deputies that never attended the meetings that were held at the Convention. They either declined or just neglected their duty.

ANSWER # 66

Benjamin Franklin has been referred to as the "Sage of the Constitution."

QUESTION # 67

Was Thomas Jefferson present at the
Constitutional Convention?

QUESTION # 68

Does the Constitution create a
Democratic form of government?

ANSWER # 67

Thomas Jefferson was not present at the Constitutional Convention because he was overseas representing America as the American Minister to France.

ANSWER # 68

The Constitution of the United States creates a Republican form of government.

QUESTION # 69

Besides the Declaration of Independence, what other contribution did Thomas Jefferson make to the Constitution of the United States?

QUESTION # 70

When was the 12th Amendment proposed by the Congress and ratified by the states?

ANSWER # 69

Besides writing the Declaration of
Independence, Thomas Jefferson
contributed the Bill of Rights – which
consists of the first 10 amendments to the
Constitution.

ANSWER # 70

The 12th Amendment was proposed by
Congress on December 9, 1803 and
eventually ratified by the requisite number of
state legislatures on June 15, 1804. It
replaced Article II, sec 1, cl 3 which changed
how the Electoral College elects the President
and the Vice-President.

QUESTION # 71

Where did the term the "United States of America" originate from?

QUESTION # 72

Which President secured the Journal and other papers of James Madison by paying a sum of money appropriated from Congress so that these artifacts could be safeguarded for posterity?

ANSWER # 71

The first known use of the formal term
"United States of America" was used was
in the Declaration of Independence.

ANSWER # 72

President Andrew Jackson paid $30,000
for James Madison's Journal and other
papers in 1837 so that these artifacts could
be safeguarded for posterity. He
appropriated the money from Congress.

QUESTION # 73

Based on the Constitution of the United States, how often must Congress assemble by law?

QUESTION # 74

According to Article IV, sec. 3, cl. 2, are delegates from U.S. Territories allowed to vote in the House or the Senate?

ANSWER # 73

Article 1, Section 4 of the Constitution of the United States requires that Congress must assemble at least once a year.

ANSWER # 74

According to the Constitution, a delegate from each organized territory may only sit in the House of Representatives. They have the right to speak on any topic and sit on committees. However, they do not have the right to vote.

QUESTION # 75

Does the Supreme Court have a power
granted by the Constitution to nullify any
act or law enacted by Congress?

QUESTION # 76

There are eight Supreme Court Justices
and one Chief Justice at the present time.
Was the number of Justices of the
Supreme Court set by the Constitution?

ANSWER # 75

> **According to the Constitution, the Supreme Court cannot nullify any law enacted by Congress. When the Court makes a decision, it only states whether the law under review is constitutional or not. If it determines that a law is unconstitutional, then it is no law.**

ANSWER # 76

> The Chief Justice alone is mentioned in the Constitution; no numbers are mentioned. The initial act of 1789 provided for a Chief Justice and five Justices. A number of acts occurred over time that changed that number: 1807, 1837, 1863, 1866, and 1869. This last act set the number at eight Justices.

QUESTION # 77

Did any of the deputies to the
Constitutional Convention sign the
Constitution by proxy?

QUESTION # 78

How are the powers not specifically
enumerated in the Constitution as powers
of the federal government assigned to the
States?

ANSWER # 77

John Dickinson of Delaware left the Constitutional Convention early due to illness. He asked his friend and fellow deputy from Delaware to sign his name to the Constitution in his absence. Later, John Dickinson was to right many letters that showed his support for the Constitution.

ANSWER # 78

The 9th and 10th Amendments of the Constitution state that the powers not specifically enumerated in the Constitution as powers of the federal government are automatically transferred to the states.

QUESTION # 79

Who are the three delegates who refused to sign the Constitution and what were their reasons?

QUESTION # 80

What became of the three non-signers of the Constitution – Elbridge Gerry of Massachusetts, George Mason of Virginia and Edmund Randolph of Virginia?

ANSWER # 79

> **The three delegates who refused to sign the Constitution were Elbridge Gerry (MA) - no Bill of Rights, George Mason (VA) – no states rights, and Edmund Randolph (VA) –checks and balances were not sufficient.**

ANSWER # 80

> Elbridge Gerry became the 5th VEEP of U.S. and died 1½ years after taking office – one of few VEEP not to run for President ; Geo. Mason joined James Madison as "Father of Bill of Rights" after it was ratified in 1791; Edmund Randolph became 1st Attorney General and 2nd Secretary of State.

QUESTION # 81

Was George Washington present at the
Philadelphia Convention to sign the
Constitution of the United States?

QUESTION # 82

How many pages are there in the
Constitution of the United States?

ANSWER # 81

Not only was George Washington present at the Philadelphia Convention to sign the Constitution, he was the President of the Convention and the first one to put his signature on this auspicious document.

ANSWER # 82

Six pages make up the Constitution of the United States – the first 4 are the 7 Articles of actual Constitution, the 5th page is a letter of transmittal and the 6th page is made up of the Bill of Rights.

QUESTION # 83

Before the 16th Amendment which was ratified in 1913, how did the federal government pay for itself?

QUESTION # 84

How many words are there in the Constitution of the United States?

ANSWER # 83

Before the 16ᵗʰ Amendment which introduced the Income Tax, the federal government amassed money by import duties, excise taxes and taxes divided amongst the states based on population.

ANSWER # 84

There are 4,543 words in the Constitution of the United States – the signatures are not included in this number.

QUESTION # 85

How long does it take on an average to read the Constitution of the United States?

QUESTION # 86

How many words are there in the Declaration of Independence?

ANSWER # 85

It takes about a half hour to read the
Constitution of the United States on
average.

ANSWER # 86

There are 1,458 words in the Declaration
of Independence?

QUESTION # 87

How long does it take to read the
Declaration of Independence?

QUESTION # 88

Who was the Penman who is responsible
for the handwritten copy of the
Constitution of the United States and how
much was he paid for his employment?

ANSWER # 87

The Declaration of Independence is slower reading than the Constitution – it takes about 10 minutes.

ANSWER # 88

The person responsible for the handwritten copy of the Constitution of the United States was an Assistant Clerk for the Pennsylvania State Assembly named Jacob Shallus. It was determined that he had an office in the State House and was probably paid $30.00 for his employment.

QUESTION # 89

Did the Assistant Clerk named Jacob Shallus who was hired to pen the first copy of the Constitution of the United States realize the importance of the document he was asked to produce?

QUESTION # 90

Which part of the Constitution of the United States gives the President the power to call a special session of Congress?

ANSWER # 89

Since Jacob Shallus died in 1796, there is a good chance that he did not realize how important a task he had performed when he penned the first copy of the Constitution of the United States.

ANSWER # 90

Article 2 of the Constitution gave the President power to call a special session of Congress. The last time it was exercised by a President was in 1947 when President Harry S. Truman called the "turnip" session to point out how inactive the Republicans were during his term as President.

QUESTION # 91

According to the Constitution, can the Secretary of State (on the behalf of the President) recognize a new government without the consent of Congress?

QUESTION # 92

What names were given to those factions that represented opposing views about ratifying the Constitution of the United States?

ANSWER # 91

According to Article II, sec. 3, the
Secretary of State (on behalf of the
President) has the power to recognize a
new government without consulting or
getting the consent of Congress.

ANSWER # 92

Those favoring ratification of the
Constitution after it was adopted were
called the Federalists – those in
opposition were referred to as Anti-
federalists.

QUESTION # 93

What part of the Constitution of the
United States prevents Congress and the
States from passing ex post facto laws?

QUESTION # 94

Were the people permitted to vote on the
ratification of the Constitution?

ANSWER # 93

The Constitution of the United States views any portion of a retroactive portion of any law as unconstitutional. Article 1, Section 9 prevents Congress from passing any ex post facto laws while Article 1, Section 10 prevents the States from passing any ex post facto laws.

ANSWER # 94

According to Article VII of the Constitution, the vote on the ratification of the Constitution was to be assigned to the State Legislatures rather than to a direct vote by all the people in the newly formed Union.

QUESTION # 95

How many States out of the thirteen states were needed in order for the Constitution to be ratified?

QUESTION # 96

What was the order in which the States ratified the Constitution?

ANSWER # 95

According to Article VII of the
Constitution, 9 States were necessary for
ratification.

ANSWER # 96

The order in which the States ratified the
Constitution of the United States is:
Delaware, Pennsylvania, New Jersey,
Georgia, Connecticut, Massachusetts,
Maryland, South Carolina, New
Hampshire, Virginia and New York.

QUESTION # 97

Since only 11 States ratified the Constitution, how did the remaining two States – Rhode Island and North Carolina react?

QUESTION # 98

What stipulation does the Constitution of the United States attach to the President's ability to sign treaties and make agreements with foreign powers?

ANSWER # 97

After the inauguration of George Washington as the 1st President of the United States, both Rhode Island and North Carolina joined the other 11 States in agreeing with the ratification of the Constitution.

ANSWER # 98

Article 2, Section 2 of the Constitution of the United States state that if the President signs treaties or makes agreements with foreign powers, then 2/3 majority of the Senate must concur.

QUESTION # 99

During the ratification process, which
states had the most heated contests?

QUESTION # 100

Which part of the Constitution of the
United States gives the President the
power to appoint Supreme Court Justices?

ANSWER # 99

During the ratification process, the States
with the most heated contests were:
Massachusetts, Virginia and New York.

ANSWER # 100

**Article II of the Constitution of the
United States gives the President the
power to appoint Supreme Court Justices.**

QUESTION # 101

What was the outcome of the vote for ratification at the State Convention of New York where there was just a margin of three votes?

QUESTION # 102

What was the outcome of the vote for ratification at the State Convention of Massachusetts?

CIVICS ANSWER # 101

With just a margin of 3 votes, the State
Convention of New York supported
ratification by a vote of 30-27.

CIVICS ANSWER # 102

The State Convention of Massachusetts
supported ratification by a vote of 168-133.

QUESTION # 103

Why did the founding fathers create the
Senate as a part of Congress?

QUESTION # 104

What was the outcome of the vote for
ratification at the State Convention of
Virginia?

ANSWER # 103

Congress created the Senate to give a greater voice to the smaller states in the Union. Its purpose was to balance the power in Congress with that of the House where the number of representatives is divided by the population.

ANSWER # 104

The State Convention of Virginia supported ratification by a vote of 89-79.

QUESTION # 105

How many Amendments were offered as a result of the State Conventions that were convened to ratify the Constitution of the United States?

QUESTION # 106

What is the term of office of the Treasurer of the United States?

ANSWER # 105

Even though there was an overlap with regard to topics covered, there were 124 amendments offered as a result of the State Conventions held to ratify the Constitution.

ANSWER # 106

According to Article I, sec 8 and Article II, 2, the President appoints the Treasurer of the United States and the length of office is for an unspecified period of time.

QUESTION # 107

Aside from judges, which government position has the longest term of office?

QUESTION # 108

What is the amount of money that a lawsuit must exceed so that a trial by jury cannot be denied?

ANSWER # 107

The Comptroller General of the United States and the Assistant Comptroller of the United States both hold their offices for fifteen years.

ANSWER # 108

According to the 7th Amendment of the Constitution of the United States, a trial by jury cannot be denied if the amount of the lawsuit under consideration exceeds $20.

QUESTION # 109

Is Education mentioned in the Constitution
of the United States?

QUESTION # 110

**Who wrote the Declaration of
Independence which came before the
Constitution of the United States?**

ANSWER # 109

There is no mention at all of Education in the Constitution of the United States because the Founding Fathers believed that Education was the responsibility of the individual States.

ANSWER # 110

The Declaration of Independence was written by Thomas Jefferson. It was a statement adopted by the Continental Congress on July 4th, 1776.

QUESTION # 111

When did the Supreme Court hold its first
session making the Judicial Branch
operational?

QUESTION # 112

**When did the Executive Branch of the
U.S. government become fully
operational?**

ANSWER # 111

The Supreme Court held its first session on February 2, 1790. It was at this time that the Judicial Branch and the government of the United States were fully operational.

ANSWER # 112

The Executive Branch became fully operational when George Washington was inaugurated on April 30, 1789.

QUESTION # 113

What provision does the Constitution of the United States make to protect the life, liberty or property of its citizens?

QUESTION # 114

When did the Legislative Branch of the U.S. government become fully operational?

ANSWER # 113

According to the 5th and 14th Amendments of the Constitution of the United States, no person shall be deprived of life, liberty or property without due process of law.

ANSWER # 114

The Legislative Branch of the U.S. government became fully operational on April 6, 1789 when both Houses were able to establish a quorum (minimal number of members of an organization, usually a majority, needed to conduct business).

QUESTION # 115

When did the old Confederation end, thereby allowing the new government to function legally?

QUESTION # 116

Was the word "veto" ever mentioned in the Constitution of the United States?

ANSWER # 115

The old Confederation ended on March 3, 1789.

ANSWER # 116

The word "veto" is never mentioned in the Constitution of the United States. James Madison used the word "negative" instead.

QUESTION # 117

When George Washington was elected President by the Electoral College, how many votes were cast and how many did he receive?

QUESTION # 118

While the Constitution of the United States guarantees each citizen the right to vote, did any amendment address discrimination with regard to this inherent right?

ANSWER # 117

George Washington received a unanimous vote for President by 69 electors (one for each elector) from the 10 states out of 13 allowed to vote. Rhode Island and North Carolina were not eligible while New York had deadlocked in the state legislature over which 8 electors to choose.

ANSWER # 118

While the 15th Amendment (ratified in 1870) states that the federal government or the states cannot deny or abridge a citizen's right to vote because of race, color or previous condition of servitude, the 18th Amendment echoes the same right. This amendment states that the right is on account of sex.

QUESTION # 119

How did the Electoral College choose the Vice-President who turned out to be John Adams?

QUESTION # 120

What happened to the other 12 votes that were available to the Electoral College (Total votes available = 81 votes; votes cast = 69 votes)?

ANSWER # 119

While George Washington ran unopposed and received 1 vote from each elector (69), each elector other vote was dispersed over the 11 nominees who ran for VEEP. The electors intentionally voted for others in order to deny John Adams the unanimous vote that George Washington had received.

ANSWER # 120

The 12 votes not cast are divided: Rhode Island (2 votes) and North Carolina (2 votes) were not eligible to cast their votes since they had not ratified the Constitution; New York (8 votes) had deadlocked in the state legislature over who would be an elector.

QUESTION # 121

Where did the inauguration Presidential ceremony take place and who was present?

QUESTION # 122

Who administered the presidential oath of office to George Washington on the 2nd floor balcony of Federal Hall in New York City on April 30, 1789?

ANSWER # 121

On April 30, 1789 at Federal Hall (NYC), the inauguration began in the Senate chambers with the House present. After being announced by the already sworn in Vice-President John Adams, he proceeded to the 2nd floor balcony where the crowds outside could witness the swearing-in ceremony.

ANSWER # 122

The oath of office for President Elect George Washington was administered in the first capital of the United States, New York City, by the Chancellor of New York, Robert Livingston.

QUESTION # 123

According to the Constitution of the United States, who has the right to govern that part of the military employed in the service of the United States?

QUESTION # 124

Was there an Inaugural Ball scheduled for the 1st President of the United States, George Washington?

ANSWER #123

Article 1, Section 8 of the Constitution of the United States, Congress shall have the power for organizing, arming and disciplining the Militia and for governing that part of the military employed in the service of the United States.

ANSWER # 124

Although there had no Inaugural Ball scheduled on April 30, 1789 when George Washington was sworn into office in the first capital, New York City, an Inaugural Ball was scheduled for a week later on May 7, 1789 in New York City.

QUESTION # 125

What event had been scheduled after the Inauguration ceremony was complete?

QUESTION # 126

When the religious ceremony ended on Inauguration Day at St. Paul's Chapel in downtown New York City, what was the next event on the schedule?

ANSWER # 125

Once the Inauguration ceremony was complete, the entire group of attendees proceeded to St. Paul's Chapel in downtown New York City for a religious ceremony to be conducted by the Chaplin of Congress.

ANSWER # 126

When the religious ceremony at St. Paul's Chapel (a blessing on the inauguration of the newly elected President, George Washington) was ended, an assigned committee accompanied the newly-elected President to his home.

QUESTION # 127

When was the Vice-President, John Adams, sworn into office?

QUESTION # 128

Which amendment to the Constitution limits the number of terms of office a president may serve?

ANSWER # 127

Vice President John Adams was sworn
into his office on April 6th, 1789.

ANSWER # 128

Term limits for the president are
determined by the 22nd Amendment. Not
only must the president be 35 years-old
and a naturalized citizen who has lived in
the country for 14 years. They can only
serve two terms.

QUESTION # 129

When did the Supreme Court convene its first case and who was the 1st Chief Justice to preside over this new court?

QUESTION # 130

What is the 11th Amendment and how did an early Supreme Court case, Chisholm versus Georgia, prompt Congress to propose it?

ANSWER # 129

The first case of the Supreme Court
convened on February 2, 1790.

ANSWER # 130

When the Supreme Court found that the
federal judiciary could hear lawsuits against
states (Chisholm versus Georgia), Congress
proposed the 11th Amendment which was
eventually ratified (1795); it granted states
immunity for certain types of lawsuits in
federal courts.

QUESTION # 131

What were the different locations that the Supreme Court had before Chief Justice William Howard Taft won his argument in 1929 that the Supreme Court should have its own headquarters and distance itself from Congress as an independent branch of government?

QUESTION # 132

What was the last location of the Supreme Court before it moved to its present location in the structure referred to as the Supreme Court Building?

ANSWER # 131

The first location of the Supreme Court was in the Merchants Exchange Building in NYC. It then occupied Independence Hall and City Hall when the capital moved to Philadelphia, PA. In Washington, D.C., it occupied the basement of the Capital Building until it evacuated from the British in 1812.

ANSWER # 132

The last location of the Supreme Court (before it moved to its present location) was the Old Senate Chambers (presently referred to). The Supreme Court had been there since 1860. It had been in Washington all along with the exception of 1812-1819 when the capital was destroyed in the War of 1812.

QUESTION # 133

How many Chief Justices have there been since the first Chief Justice John Jay (1789) and who is the present Chief Justice of the Supreme Court?

QUESTION # 134

Does the Constitution require the Chief Justice or any Supreme Court Justice to administer the oath of office to the President on January 20th, Inauguration Day?

ANSWER # 133

Since Chief Justice John Jay was nominated by President George Washington, there have been 17 Chief Justices ending with our present-day Chief Justice, John Glover Roberts, Jr.

ANSWER # 134

The Constitution of the United States requires that the President of the United States take an oath of office. It makes no provision as to who may administer the oath of office. Traditionally, it has been the Chief Justice – but there have been exceptions due to deaths, assassinations, etc.

QUESTION # 135

Upon the death of President Warren Harding, Calvin Coolidge was administered the oath of office by his father, a notary public who was legally permitted to administer oaths and affirmations. Was this legally permitted with respect to the Presidential oath?

QUESTION # 136

While the impeachment process is initiated in the House and the trial is carried out in the Senate, are members of Congress (the House of Representatives and the Senate) allowed to be impeached?

ANSWER # 135

Despite the fact that this oath was legally sound, President Calvin Coolidge had the oath re-administered by Judge Adolph A. Hoehling of the District of Columbia Supreme Court when he returned to Washington. He did it again because the first oath had been contested.

ANSWER # 136

According to the Constitution, members of Congress cannot be impeached. They face expulsion instead of impeachment which is a formal process initiated in the House whereby a civil official is accused of unlawful activity, tried in the Senate and may be subsequently removed from office.

QUESTION # 137

If an impeachment is similar to an indictment in criminal law and does not necessarily result in conviction or immediate removal from office (it is only a statement of charges), what is the next step in the impeachment process?

QUESTION # 138

What are the 3 qualifications for becoming a member of the House of Representatives?

ANSWER # 137

Impeachment (only a legal statement of charges) usually requires a second vote by a legislative body (usually a supermajority vote) to determine whether removal from office and prevention of future office holding in a jurisdiction is warranted.

ANSWER # 138

In order to run for the House of Representatives, one must be 25 years-old, live in the district to be represented and be a U.S. citizen for 7 years.

QUESTION # 139

Who administers the oath of office to Chief Justices and Associative Justices of the Supreme Court (also known as the High Court or by its acronym SCOTUS)?

QUESTION # 140

What did the Judicial Act of 1789 specify in the year of the Court's creation?

ANSWER # 139

The oath of office is usually administered to the Chief Justice by the senior most senior Associate Justice while the Chief Justice administers the oath of office to the Associate Justice.

ANSWER # 140

The Judiciary Act of 1789 defined the Court's original and appellate jurisdiction, created 13 judicial districts and fixed the number of Associate Justices at six (beside the Chief Justice). There have been 111 Associate Justices since the Court's inception.

QUESTION # 141

If a President is impeached by the House (indicted) and goes to the Senate for a trial with the Senators acting as jurors, who presides over this trial?

QUESTION # 142

What is the difference between an impeachment (which deals with misconduct by high public officers) and criminal processes (which deal with personal misconduct) and civil processes (which deal with personal fault)?

ANSWER # 141

After the House has impeached a President and the proceedings have moved to the Senate where the Senators act as jurors, the Chief Justice of the Supreme Court shall preside over the trial.

ANSWER # 142

According to the Constitution, an impeachment is a formal process that protects the country from leadership that has become a danger due to corruption, neglect of duty, abuse of power or subversion of the Constitution of the United States.

QUESTION # 143

What body of government has the right to raise, borrow, and coin money?

QUESTION # 144

Do members of Congress (the House and Senate) receive any extra money when they serve on committees?

ANSWER # 143

> **In Section 8, the Congress shall have power to lay and collect taxes, duties, imposts and excises, to pay the debts and provide for the common defense and general welfare of the United States.**

ANSWER # 144

A

> **Members of Congress do not receive any extra money when they sit on committees since this is part of the job description of their posts.**

QUESTION # 145

Are members of the President's Cabinet permitted to sit in Congress (House and Senate) at the same time and hold concurrent positions?

QUESTION # 146

According to the Constitution, where must bills that raise revenue and bills that appropriate money be enacted?

ANSWER # 145

Members appointed to a President's Cabinet are not permitted to also hold concurrent positions as members of Congress (House and Senate).

ANSWER # 146

According to the Constitution, all bills that raise revenue must be enacted in the House of Representatives whereas all bills that appropriate money should be enacted in the House – but can be enacted in the Senate.

QUESTION # 147

Can the Senate ever vote to adjourn or suspend an impeachment trial during the impeachment process?

QUESTION # 148

What are the qualifications to become a Senator according to the Constitution of the United States?

ANSWER # 147

Yes - the Senate needs a simple majority
(51 out of 100 votes) to adjourn, suspend
or seek other alternatives at any time
during the impeachment process.

ANSWER # 148

To become a U.S. Senator, one must be
30 years-old, a resident of the state
represented at the time of taking office
and a U.S. citizen for 9 years.

QUESTION # 149

If the President vetoes (veto – Latin – "to forbid") legislation, what recourse does Congress have according to the Constitution?

QUESTION # 150

How is a "Pocket Veto" (which is a legislative maneuver in federal lawmaking that allows a President to indirectly veto a bill) exercised?

ANSWER # 149

If the President vetoes legislation proposed by Congress, Congress has the power to override this veto with a 2/3 vote in both houses (the House and the Senate).

ANSWER # 150

According to Article I, sec 7, if a Congress by its own adjournment prevents the return of a bill by the President, the bill is deemed not to be a law. This constitutes a pocket veto.

Books by James Magee

<u>I Know Stuff</u> (fiction)

<u>The Guy from Brooklyn</u>

<u>Let No Man Write My Epitaph</u>

<u>USS Okinawa (LPH-3)</u>

<u>From Submersibles to Nuclear Submarines</u>

<u>A Brief History of Chess</u>

<u>100 Memorable Movie Plots and Dialogue</u>

<u>101 Memorable Movie Plots</u>

<u>102 Memorable Movie Plots</u>

<u>103 Memorable Movie Plots</u>

<u>American History</u>

<u>World History</u>

<u>The Fifty States</u>

<u>World Capitals</u>

<u>Understanding Legal Terms/Courtroom Humor</u>

<u>Classic/Muscle Car Trivia</u>

<u>The History of the Novel: Six Literary Periods</u>

<u>The History of Drama: Playwrights and Their Plays</u>

<u>The History of Opera: Composers and Their Operas</u>

<u>Misspell or Misspell?</u>

Shakespeare Unplugged

The Triple Crown Affair: Horseracing Basics

Basic Accounting and Finance Quiz

Psychology 101 – Part I

Psychology 101 – Part II

Philosophy 101

A Simple Guide to Philosophy

Art History Review

Music History Review

Rock 'n Roll Review

Motown/Female Groups/British Invasion

Classic Novels (Authors and Their Titles)

The Opening and Closing Lines of Novels

Classical Novels (Start . . . Finish)

Who Wrote This Book?

Novel Characters of Literature

Fictional Characters of Literature

The Constitution of the United States – America's Owner's Manual

www.ingramcontent.com/pod-product-compliance
Lightning Source LLC
Chambersburg PA
CBHW070833310526
45788CB00017B/561